IT Operator

IT Operators perform day-to-day
include performing backups, co
scheduled tasks.

CW00719828

3.4.4 Application Manager

Application Manager/Team-leader

Each application team or department has an Application Manager or
Team-leader, responsible for leadership, decision making, team training
and awareness, communications with users and customers, and reporting
to senior management.

Application Analyst/Architect

Application Analysts/Architects are responsible for matching requirements
to application specifications. Activities include working with stakeholders
to understand their needs, ensuring that applications are designed
to be managed effectively and helping to generate acceptance test
requirements.

3.4.5 Event Management roles

Most organizations do not have an 'Event Manager' as events are managed
in many different contexts. Event Management procedures must, however,
be coordinated.

Technical/Application Management

Technical and Application Management participate in the design of
instrumentation, event classification, correlation engines and auto
responses. They usually help in testing Event Management and may have
responsibility for monitoring systems.

IT Operations Management

IT Operations Management is usually responsible for monitoring events and taking appropriate actions. This activity is often carried out by an operations bridge.

3.4.6 Incident Management roles

Incident Manager

The Incident Manager is the process owner for the Incident Management Process, responsible for the efficiency and effectiveness of the process, making recommendations for improvement and developing and maintaining the supporting systems, processes and procedures.

First-line support

First-line support is usually provided by the Service Desk, and is responsible for logging and managing Incidents and, if authorized, may resolve and close Incidents where it can.

Second-line support

Second-line support is responsible for investigating Incidents where more time or skills are required. This group is often located with the Service Desk.

Third-line support

Third-line support is generally provided by personnel from Technical Management, or from suppliers, with focus on specific technologies.

3.4.7 Request Fulfilment roles

Handling of Service Requests is usually carried out by Service Desk and Incident Management staff.

Service Operation teams may be responsible for fulfilling specific requests, and other functions such as procurement, and facilities management may also play a role.

3.4.8 Problem Management roles

The Problem Manager is the process owner for the Problem Management process.

The Problem Manager also deals with problem-solving groups, ensures that Known Errors are effectively managed, manages communication with suppliers and external groups needed to help solve Problems and carries out major Problem reviews.

Problem-solving groups, responsible for the actual solving of Problems, are usually part of Technical Management, Application Management or suppliers.

3.4.9 Access Management roles

Access Management roles should be defined by the Information Security Management and Application Management areas.

Service Desk

The Service Desk is typically used to log Access Requests, and carry out validation before passing them to an appropriate team.

Technical/Application Management

Technical and Application Management ensure that mechanisms are created to control Access Management, test the service to ensure that access controls are effective, and perform Access Management for systems under their control.

IT Operations Management

IT Operations Management commonly provides and revokes access to systems or resources, following instructions within standard operating procedures.

3.5 SERVICE OPERATION PROCESSES

3.5.1 Event Management

Definition of an event

An event may indicate that something is not functioning correctly, leading to an Incident being logged. Some events do not require any action to be taken. For example, a user logging in may be recorded, but not require any further activity.

Event Management provides the ability to detect events, to make sense of them, and to determine the appropriate control activity. This may require human intervention, but it may be automated.

Event Management depends on monitoring, but the two are different. Event Management generates and detects meaningful notifications. Monitoring checks the status of components even when no events are occurring.

The scope of Event Management includes detecting failures or changes of state in Configuration Items (CIs), detecting environmental conditions such as fire and smoke, monitoring licence usage and logging normal activities such as server performance.

The Event Management process includes the steps shown in Figure 3.1.

Figure 3.1 Event Management process flow

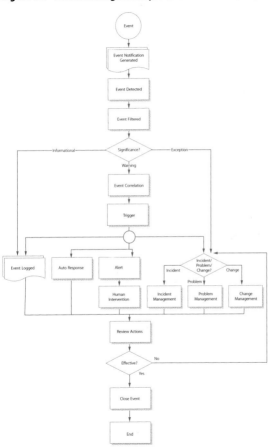

Event occurrence, notification and detection

Everybody involved in designing, developing and supporting services and infrastructure must understand what events need to be detected. This is used to design instrumentation. Notification and detection can take one of two forms: either the CI generates a notification and sends it to a suitable destination, or a management tool collects data and reports the event.

Notification data and responsibilities are documented during Service Design and Service Transition, to ensure that the appropriate staff are notified of events and can take appropriate actions.

Event filtering and significance

Filtering decides whether to take further action. For example, it may be impossible to disable event notifications that are unwanted.

Significance of an event may be one of:

■ Information – no action required; the event is logged; e.g. a user logging in, or a batch job completing successfully
■ Warning – a threshold is being approached and a person, process or tool should be notified to enable appropriate action to be taken; e.g. high CPU utilization, or an increase in soft errors on a disk
■ Exception alert – a service or CI is operating abnormally; this may mean that an Incident has occurred or, for example, the detection of a normal event such as the addition of a component as part of a planned change.

Event correlation

To understand an event, it is important to understand what other events have occurred, which other CIs are generating events, etc. This analysis is usually done by a 'correlation engine' within a management tool. Correlation engine configuration is based on standards created during Service Design.

Trigger and response selection

A trigger initiates a response. The trigger could be logging an Incident, running a script, paging a system administrator or support personnel, etc.

The response could be one of the following:

- Event logged – the event should be logged, even if no other action is required; the log could be maintained within the Event Management tool, or on the device or system being monitored
- Auto response – an event may be understood well enough that the response can be automated, e.g. a server reboot, service restart or locking an application to prevent unauthorized access
- Alert and human intervention – an alert ensures that a person with appropriate skills deals with an Incident, Problem or change; some events need to be managed through the Incident, Problem or Change Management processes.

Review and close

It is not usually possible to review every event as there may be very large numbers. It is important to check that significant events have been handled properly. This is often done as part of the review of the related Incident, Problem or change.

Some events are closed automatically, when the Event Management tool detects that the issue has been resolved. Before manually closing an event, it should be linked to any related Incident or Problem record, where appropriate.

3.5.2 Incident Management

Definition of an Incident

An Incident is an unplanned interruption to an IT service, or reduction in the quality of an IT service. Failure of a configuration item that has not yet impacted service is also an Incident.

The purpose of Incident Management is to restore normal service as quickly as possible, and to minimize the adverse impact on business operations.

The scope of Incident Management includes any event that disrupts, or could disrupt, a service. This includes events that are communicated by users, as well as Incidents detected and reported by technical staff or monitoring tools.

Timescales must be agreed for all stages of Incident handling, based on priority. Incident models can help ensure that standard approaches are followed and timescales are met – for example, for managing security Incidents, or using well-defined solutions for common types of Incident. Major Incidents should have a separate procedure, with shorter timescales and greater urgency.

The Incident Management process includes the steps shown in Figure 3.2.

Figure 3.2 Incident Management process flow

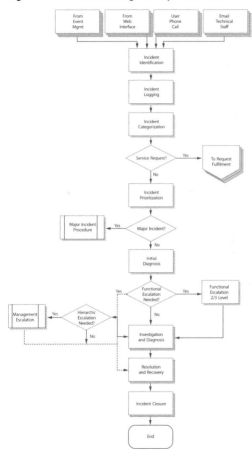

Incident identification and logging

Incidents must be identified as early as possible. It is best for this to be done by monitoring and Event Management. Some Incidents will be logged by users contacting the Service Desk.

It is good practice to provide a self-help tool to allow users to log Incidents using a web-based, menu-driven system if possible. This can also be used to allow users to check the status of Incidents and provide updates.

All Incidents must be logged and date/time stamped. The log must include all information needed to manage the Incident, and be updated and maintained throughout the life of the Incident.

Incident categorization

The Service Desk often handles Service Requests as well as Incidents, so these must be identified and managed through the Request Fulfilment process.

Categories are assigned to identify which groups may need to be involved in helping to resolve the Incident, and for trend analysis.

Resolution times, based on Incident priority, are usually documented in Service Level Agreements (SLAs), and are often automatically generated by Incident Management tools.

Initial diagnosis and escalation

Initial diagnosis is usually carried out by Service Desk Analysts. Diagnostic scripts may be used to discover information and identify Known Errors.

If possible, the Service Desk Analyst will resolve and close the Incident while the user is still on the phone, otherwise they may carry out further investigation or they may escalate the Incident.

If a greater level of technical expertise is needed, functional escalation is used to pass the Incident to a technical support team with appropriate skills. If a greater level of management involvement is needed, hierarchic escalation is used to engage appropriate levels of management.

Investigation and diagnosis

Support teams perform investigation and diagnosis. If multiple teams are involved, they may work in parallel to speed up the process, but activities must be coordinated.

Investigation includes actions such as establishing exactly what happened, the order of events, number and relationships of CIs affected and what could have triggered the Incident. Diagnosis often includes searching Incident and Problem records and Known Error Databases (KEDBs) and, most importantly, what can be done to restore service.

Resolution, recovery and closure

When a potential resolution to the Incident has been identified, it is applied and tested and the service is restored to the users.

The Incident should not be closed until it is resolved to the user's satisfaction. At this time, the Incident category is checked and a closure category assigned; satisfaction surveys are conducted; checks are made to ensure that the Incident has been fully documented and to decide whether a Problem should be logged.

3.5.3 Request Fulfilment

Definition of a Service Request

A Service Request is a request from a user for information or advice, a standard change or access to an IT service.

The purpose of Request Fulfilment is to enable users to request and receive standard services; to source and deliver these services; to provide information to users and customers about services and procedures for obtaining them; and to assist with general information, complaints and comments.

The scope of Request Fulfilment varies in different organizations. Some organizations have an Incident type of 'service request' and use the Incident Management process to manage them, but, if there are many Service Requests, it is better to have a distinct process. In each case, it is important that the process used to manage Service Requests is clearly documented.

Service Requests are usually changes, but, because of their small scale and frequent, low-cost, low-risk nature, it is better to have a separate process so that the Change Management process does not become overloaded.

Many types of Service Requests occur frequently and must be handled in a consistent manner. This is achieved by using pre-defined Request Models, pre-approved by Change Management.

The Service Request process includes the following steps.

Menu selection

The most common way to log Service Requests is via a self-help menu system. It is possible to log requests using other routes into the Service Desk, such as phone calls, but a web-based, 'shopping basket'-style front-end has many advantages.

Financial and other approval

Most requests will have some form of financial implication. The cost of fulfilling the request must be established; this will be done in advance for many types of request, and the cost must be presented to the user or their management. If approval is given, the process may need to include charging.

In some cases – such as compliance-related or wider business approval – further approval may be needed.

Fulfilment and closure

Some simple requests may be completed by the Service Desk; others will be forwarded to specialist groups or suppliers.

There may be specialized groups responsible for fulfilling some types of request, or these may even be outsourced to third parties. Regardless of who carries out the actual work, the Service Desk should monitor progress and keep users informed.

When the request has been fulfilled, it should be referred back to the Service Desk for closure, following a very similar process to that for Incident closure.

3.5.4   Access Management

Access Management helps to manage confidentiality, availability and integrity of data and intellectual property; it is the operation of parts of Availability and Information Security Management.

Access Management activities are often performed by Technical and Application Management functions, and coordinated by IT Operations Management or the Service Desk.

Access Management uses a number of technical terms, including:

- **Access** – the functionality or data to which a user is entitled
- **Identity** – unique information that distinguishes an individual user
- **Rights** – settings that provide a user with access to services
- **Services** or **Service Groups** – things to which access is granted
- **Directory Services** – a tool and database used to manage access and rights.

The Access Management process includes the following stages.

Requesting access

Common ways to request access include:

- Submitting a Request for Change (RFC)
- A standard change request generated by a human resources (HR) department system
- A Service Request from the Request Fulfilment process
- Executing a pre-authorized script or option.

Verification

Every request for access must be verified in order to:

- Confirm the identity of the user – this can be achieved with a user name and password, but, for sensitive services, may also require biometrics, electronic access keys or other means of identification
- Ensure that the user has a legitimate requirement for the service – this usually requires independent verification, such as notification from HR, authorization from a pre-defined manager, or a policy that specifies user access rights.

When a new service is released, the Change record should specify which users or groups of users will have access.

Providing rights

Access Management does not decide who may access which service; it just executes policies and regulations defined during Service Strategy and Service Design.

Access Management should regularly review roles and groups to ensure that they are appropriate.

Monitoring identity status

User roles sometimes change, and so do their needs to access services. Examples of role changes include job changes, promotions, transfers, resignation, retirement and dismissal.

Access Management should document the typical User Lifecycle for each type of user, and tools should provide features that enable a user to be moved between states and groups.

Logging and tracking access

Access Management ensures that rights are used properly. This Access Monitoring and Control may be performed by Technical and Application Management.

Exceptions may be handled by Incident Management, using an Incident Model for abuse of access rights. These Incident records should have restricted access to avoid exposing vulnerabilities.

Records of access to services may be needed during forensic investigations. Evidence may be needed of dates, times and even content of a user's access to a specific service.

Removing or restricting rights

Access Management is responsible for revoking access rights after changes such as resignation, dismissal or change of job role or death.

On some occasions, access rights or times might need changing without completely revoking access, e.g. if a user is temporarily reassigned or has changed roles and needs a different level of access.

3.5.5 Problem Management

Definition of a Problem

A Problem is a cause of one or more Incidents. The cause is not usually known at the time a Problem record is created, and the Problem Management process is responsible for further investigation.

The scope of Problem Management includes diagnosing causes of Incidents, determining the resolution and ensuring that this is implemented. Implementation usually involves Change and Release Management. Problem Management is also responsible for preventing Problems and recurring Incidents, and minimizing the impact of Incidents that cannot be prevented.

Problem Management maintains information about Problems, workarounds and resolutions, and so has a strong link with Knowledge Management. Problem Management usually uses the same tools as Incident Management, and similar categorization, impact and priority coding systems.

Problem Models can be used to help ensure consistent handling of similar types of Problem.

Reactive Problem Management is part of Service Operation; proactive Problem Management is the activity in Continual Service Improvement that identifies Problems based on analysis of Incident data.

The Problem Management process includes the steps shown in Figure 3.3.

IT Operator

IT Operators perform day-to-day operational activities. These typically include performing backups, console operations, managing jobs and scheduled tasks.

3.4.4 Application Management roles

Figure 3.3 Problem Management process flow

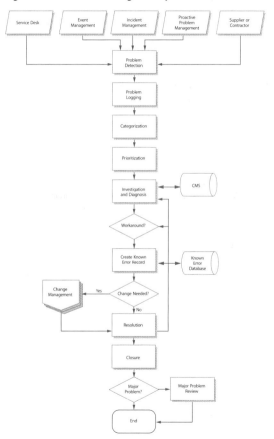

Problem detection and logging

There are many ways a Problem could be detected, including:

- The Service Desk may not know the cause of an Incident, even if they have resolved the Incident itself by applying a workaround
- A technical support group may identify that a Problem exists
- Monitoring tools may detect an infrastructure failure, which could lead to both an Incident and a Problem being identified
- Proactive Problem Management.

All Problems must be logged, and Problem records must include all the details needed to manage the Problem through its lifecycle, including links to related Incidents.

Problem categorization and prioritization

Problems are categorized to enable analysis and reporting. It is advisable to use the same coding system as for Incidents.

Problems should be prioritized in the same way and for the same reasons as Incidents. Problem priority should take into account the frequency and impact of related Incidents. Problem priority is also based on the severity of the Problem, which is a measure of how serious the Problem is from an infrastructure perspective, e.g. how long it will take to fix, or how much it will cost.

Problem investigation and diagnosis

An investigation diagnoses the cause of the Problem. The speed and nature of the investigation, and the resources invested, should depend on impact, severity and urgency of the Problem.

There are a number of useful problem-solving techniques that can be used, including:

- Chronological Analysis – documents events sorted by date and time
- Pain Value Analysis – applies a formula that accounts for number of people affected, downtime, cost to the business and other factors, to

establish to which Problems resources should be allocated
■ Kepner and Tregoe – detailed Problem definition, establish possible causes, test the most probable cause and verify the true cause
■ Thought Sharing – gets people together in one room to offer ideas on potential causes and actions
■ Ishikawa Diagrams – creates a structured diagram showing relationships between causes and effects
■ Pareto Analysis – separates important potential causes from issues that are more trivial.

Workarounds and raising Known Error Records

A workaround is a way of reducing or eliminating the impact of a Problem, but not fully resolving its cause. If a workaround has been implemented, the Problem record should remain open until the Problem has been resolved.

When diagnosis is complete, and particularly when a workaround has been found, a Known Error Record should be raised and stored in the KEDB so that further Incidents or Problems can be identified and the service restored more quickly. Sometimes it may be advantageous to raise a Known Error Record earlier in the overall process.

Problem resolution and closure

Full resolution of a Problem usually involves raising a Change Request. If the Problem is very serious, this may be an Emergency Change Request. Sometimes it may not be possible to justify the change in a business case, and a decision may be made to leave the Problem record open and rely on the workaround in the Known Error Record.

When the Problem has been resolved, the Problem record and related Incident records should be closed. The record should be checked to ensure that it contains all required information and the status of related Known Error Records should be updated.

Major Problem review

A major Problem is identified by the priority assigned to it. After a major Problem has been closed, a review should be conducted to learn lessons for the future. The review should examine things that were done correctly, and incorrectly; what could be done better; how to prevent reoccurrence; and whether follow-up to third-party actions is required.

Lessons from the review should be discussed with the customer, to help improve customer satisfaction.

3.5.6 Operational aspects of other lifecycle stages

Processes described in other stages of the Service Lifecycle also have significant operational content, as summarized below. These are all activities that Service Operation staff are involved with on a regular basis.

- **Change Management** – raising and submitting RFCs to address Service Operation issues, participation in Change Advisory Board (CAB) and Emergency CAB meetings, and implementing or backing out changes
- **Configuration Management** – informing Configuration Management of any discrepancies found between CIs and the Configuration Management System (CMS), and making any amendments necessary to correct such discrepancies
- **Release and Deployment Management** – performing actual implementations, participation in the planning stages of major releases to advise on Service Operation issues and physical handling of CIs from/to the Definitive Media Library (DML)
- **Capacity Management** – capacity planning, modelling and application sizing, capacity and performance monitoring, handling related Incidents, collecting and storing capacity and performance data, and identifying trends
- **Availability Management** – IT services are designed for availability and recovery during Service Design; Service Operation is responsible for making the service available to the specified users at the required

time and agreed levels; the operational stage is when IT teams and users are in the best position to detect whether services meet requirements and whether the design of these services is effective

■ **Knowledge Management** – it is essential that all data and information needed for future Service Operation activities are properly gathered, stored and assessed; relevant data, metrics and information should be passed to management and to other service lifecycle phases so that it can feed into the knowledge and wisdom layers of the organization's Service Knowledge Management System (SKMS)

■ **IT Service Continuity Management (ITSCM)** – Service Operation functions are responsible for the testing and execution of recovery plans, as determined in the organization's IT Service Continuity plans; it is important that Service Operation staff contribute to the Business Continuity Central Coordination team and take part in activities such as Risk Assessment, and the writing of recovery plans for systems and services under their control.

3.6 SERVICE OPERATION COMMON ACTIVITIES

Section 3.5 introduced the processes required for effective Service Operation, and section 3.7 deals with some of the organizational aspects. This section focuses on a number of operational activities that ensure that technology is aligned with the overall service and process objectives.

Managing technology

It is impossible to achieve quality services without aligning and 'gearing' every level of technology (and the people who manage it) to the services being provided. Service Management involves people, process and technology.

3.6.1 Monitoring and control

The measurement and control of services is based on a continual cycle of monitoring, reporting and subsequent action. This cycle is fundamental to the delivery, support and improvement of services – and, although it takes place during Service Operation, it provides a basis for setting strategy, designing and testing services and achieving meaningful improvement.

Definition of monitoring
Monitoring refers to the activity of observing a situation to detect changes that happen over time.

Monitoring, in the context of Service Operation, will typically involve the use of tools to check the status of IT services, key CIs and key operational activities, and to track and record their output and performance.

Definition of reporting
Reporting refers to the analysis, production and distribution of the output of the monitoring activity.

The output of monitoring needs to be collated and disseminated to appropriate groups, functions or processes for interpretation and decision making.

Definition of control
Control refers to the process of managing the utilization or behaviour of a device, system or service. It is important to note that simply manipulating a device is not the same as controlling it.

The performance of devices, systems or services will be regulated and any required corrective action taken. Control will again utilize tools to define which conditions represent normal operations or abnormal operations.

Monitor Control Loops

The most common model for defining control is the Monitor Control Loop. Although it is a simple concept, it has many complex applications within ITSM.

Figure 3.4 outlines the basic principles of control.

Figure 3.4 The Monitor Control Loop

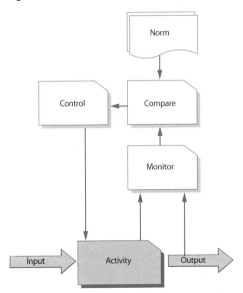

A single activity and its output are measured using a pre-defined norm, or standard, to determine whether it is within an acceptable range of performance or quality. If not, action is taken to rectify the situation or to restore normal performance.

Typically, there are two types of Monitor Control Loops:

- **Open Loop Systems** – designed to perform a specific activity regardless of environmental conditions, e.g. a backup can be initiated at a given time and frequency, and will run regardless of other conditions
- **Closed Loop Systems** – monitor an environment and respond to changes in that environment, e.g. in network load balancing, a monitor will evaluate the traffic on a circuit and, if network traffic exceeds a certain range, the control system will begin to route traffic across a backup circuit.

To help clarify the difference, solving Capacity Management through over-provisioning is open loop; a load-balancer that detects congestion/failure and redirects capacity is closed loop.

Figure 3.5 illustrates a Complex Monitor Control Loop. The diagram shows a process that has three major activities, each with an input and output. The output of one activity becomes an input for the next.

Figure 3.5 Complex Monitor Control Loop

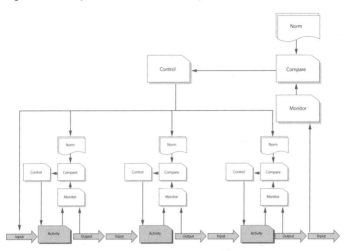

Complex Monitor Control Loops can be used to operate IT services and ITSM as a whole. Such loops can be used to manage the:

■ Performance of activities in a process or procedure
■ Effectiveness of a process or procedure as a whole, e.g. Change Management will measure the success of the process by checking whether a change was implemented on time, to specification and within budget
■ Performance of a device, e.g. the 'activity' box could represent the response time of a server under a given workload
■ Performance of a series of devices, e.g. the end-user response time of an application across the network.

3.6.2 Service Operation specific activities

There are many activities carried out by personnel working for Service Operation functions. These activities are not part of formal processes, but need to be reliably performed.

Some of these activities involve the management of specific technology platforms, and these all include procurement advice, installation support, ongoing housekeeping and maintenance, monitoring, third-level support for any related Incidents/Problems, licence management, capacity and performance, and decommissioning.

Console management/operations bridge

These provide a central coordination point for monitoring and managing IT services and infrastructure. This includes the management of events, detecting Incidents, managing routine operational activities and reporting on the status or performance of technology components.

These activities are usually undertaken from a single location, often known as the operations bridge, and include console management, event handling, first-line network management, job scheduling and out-of-hours support (covering for the Service Desk and/or second-line support groups if they do not work 24/7).

Job scheduling

Job scheduling involves defining and initiating job-scheduling software packages to run batch and real-time work. This will normally involve daily, weekly, monthly, annual and ad hoc schedules to meet business needs.

Backup and restore

The organization's data has to be protected, and this will include backup and storage of data in remote locations where it can be protected – available for restore due to any loss, corruption or implementation of IT Service Continuity plans.

An overall backup strategy needs to be agreed with the business, covering the data that has to be backed up, the frequency of backup, the number of generations to be retained, storage locations, etc.

Print and output

Many services consist of generating and delivering information in printed or electronic form. Ensuring the right information gets to the right people, with full integrity, requires formal control and management.

Mainframe management

Mainframes are still in use and have mature practices. Mainframes form the central component of many services, and their performance sets a baseline for service performance and user or customer expectations.

Server management and support

Servers are used in most organizations to provide flexible and accessible services, such as hosting applications or databases, running client/server services, storage, print and file management. Successful management of servers is therefore essential for successful Service Operation.

Network Management

Network Management is responsible for the organization's local area networks (LANs), metropolitan area networks (MANs) and wide area networks (WANs) – and for liaising with third-party network suppliers.

Storage and archive

Many services require the storage of data for specific timescales, both online and offline. This is often due to regulatory or legislative requirements, but also because history and audit data are invaluable for a variety of purposes, including marketing, product development, forensic investigations, etc.

Database Administration

Database Administration works closely with key Application Management teams or departments and aims to ensure the optimal performance, security and functionality of databases that it manages.

Directory services management

A directory service is a specialized software application that manages information about the resources available on a network and which users have access to those resources. It is the basis for providing access to the resources and for ensuring that unauthorized access is detected and prevented.

Desktop support

As most users access IT services using desktop or laptop computers, it is key that these are supported to ensure the agreed levels of availability and performance of services. Desktop support will have overall responsibility for all of the organization's desktop and laptop computer hardware, software and peripherals.

Middleware management

Middleware is software that connects or integrates software components across distributed or disparate applications and systems. Middleware enables the effective transfer of data between applications, and is key to services that are dependent on multiple applications or data sources.

Internet/web management

Many organizations conduct much of their business through the Internet and are therefore heavily dependent upon the availability and performance of their websites. In such cases, a separate Internet/Web Support team or department may be desirable and justified.

Facilities and data centre management

Facilities management refers to the management of the physical environment, usually located in data centres or computer rooms.

The main activities of facilities management are:

- **Building management** – maintenance and upkeep of the buildings that house the IT staff and Data Centre
- **Equipment hosting** – ensures that special requirements are provided for the physical housing of equipment
- **Power management** – managing the sourcing and utilization of power
- **Environmental conditioning and alert systems** – smoke detection, fire suppression, heating and cooling
- **Safety** – compliance to legislation, standards and policies relative to the safety of employees
- **Physical access control** – ensures that only authorized personnel access the facility and that unauthorized access is detected and managed
- **Shipping and receiving** – management of all equipment, furniture, mail, etc. that leaves or enters the building
- **Contract management** – assists in managing suppliers and service providers involved in the facility
- **Maintenance** – the regular, scheduled upkeep of the facility.

3.7 SERVICE OPERATION FUNCTIONS

A function is a logical concept that refers to the people and automated measures that execute a defined process, activity or combination of processes or activities. In larger organizations, a function may be performed by several departments, teams or groups, or it may be embodied within a single organizational unit.

The Service Operation functions shown in Figure 3.6 are needed to manage the 'steady state' operational IT environment. These are logical functions and do not necessarily have to be performed by an equivalent organizational structure. This means that Technical and Application Management can be organized in any combination and into any number of departments. The second-level groupings in Figure 3.6 are examples of typical groups of activities performed by Technical Management (see section 3.6) and are not a suggested organization structure.

Figure 3.6 Service Operation functions

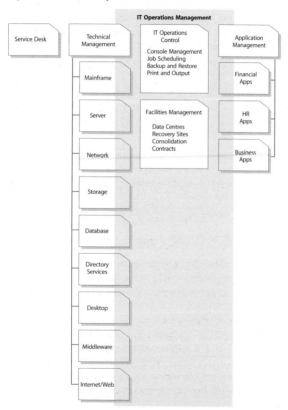

3.7.1 Service Desk

The Service Desk is a vitally important part of an organization's IT department and should be the single point of contact for IT users on a day-by-day basis. The Service Desk is key to the implementation of the Request Fulfilment and Incident Management processes described in section 3.5 and handles all Incidents and Service Requests, usually using specialist software tools to log and manage them.

A good Service Desk is often able to compensate for deficiencies elsewhere in the IT organization, but an ineffective Service Desk can give a poor impression of an otherwise very good IT organization! So, it is very important that the correct calibre of staff is used on the Service Desk and that IT Managers make it an attractive place to work in order to improve staff retention.

The primary aim of the Service Desk is to restore 'normal service' as quickly as possible. This could involve fixing an Incident, fulfilling a Service Request or answering a query – anything that is needed to allow the users to return to normal working.

Specific Service Desk responsibilities include:

- Logging all relevant Incident/Service Request details, allocating categorization and prioritization codes
- Providing first-line investigation and diagnosis
- Resolving those Incidents/Service Requests that they are able to
- Escalating Incidents/Service Requests that they cannot resolve within agreed timescales
- Keeping users informed of progress
- Closing all resolved Incidents, Requests and other calls
- Conducting customer/user satisfaction research/surveys
- Communication with users – keeping them informed of Incident progress, notifying them of impending changes or agreed outages, etc.
- Updating the CMS under the direction and approval of Configuration Management.

Service Desk organizational structure

There are many ways of structuring and locating Service Desks – and the correct solution will vary for different organizations. The exact nature of the Service Desk should be decided by the IT department in response to customer and business requirements.

The primary options are detailed below and a combination of these may be needed in order to meet fully the business needs:

- **Local Service Desk** – co-located within or physically close to the user community it serves; this often aids communication, gives a clearly visible presence, and can support local language and cultural differences, but can often be inefficient and expensive to resource as the volume and arrival rate of calls may not justify the minimum staffing levels required
- **Centralized Service Desk** – the number of Service Desks can be reduced by merging them into a single location or a smaller number of locations; this can be more efficient and cost effective, allowing fewer staff to deal with a higher volume of calls; it might still be necessary to maintain some 'local presence', but such staff can be controlled and deployed from the central desk
- **Virtual Service Desk** – through the use of technology, particularly the Internet, and corporate support tools, it is possible to give the impression of a single, centralized Service Desk when in fact the personnel may be in any number or type of locations; this gives the option of 'home working', off-shoring or outsourcing – or any combination necessary to meet user demand
- **'Follow the Sun'** – some global or international organizations may wish to combine two or more of their geographically dispersed Service Desks to provide a follow-the-sun service, which can give 24-hour coverage at relatively low cost, as no desk has to work more than a single shift; however, common processes, tools, a shared database of information, and robust handover procedures are needed for this to be successful.

Regardless of the combination of options chosen, individual users should know who to contact if they need assistance.

3.7.2   Technical Management

Technical Management refers to the groups, departments or teams that provide technical expertise and overall management of the IT infrastructure.

Technical Management plays a dual role:

- It is the custodian of technical knowledge and expertise required to manage the IT infrastructure
- It provides the actual resources to support the ITSM Lifecycle.

Technical Management also provides guidance about how best to carry out the ongoing operational management of technology.

Technical Management helps to plan, implement and maintain a stable technical infrastructure, and ensures that required resources and expertise are in place to design, build, transition, operate and improve the IT services and supporting technology.

Stability is achieved through:

- A well-designed, resilient, cost-effective infrastructure
- Use of adequate technical skills to maintain the infrastructure
- Swift use of technical skills to speedily diagnose and resolve technical failures.

Technical Management activities

Technical Management is involved in two types of activity:

- Those that are generic to the Technical Management function as a whole, in support of managing and operating the IT services and infrastructure

- A set of discrete activities and processes performed by all three functions of Technical, Application and IT Operations Management. These activities are summarized in section 3.6.

The generic Technical Management activities required to manage and operate IT service and infrastructure include:

- Identifying the knowledge and expertise required, documenting skill requirements, initiating training programmes for IT and user staff and recruiting or contracting appropriate skills
- Defining architecture standards; participating in the definition and design of technology architectures; researching and developing solutions to expand the service portfolio, automate IT operations, reduce costs or increase service levels
- Involvement in the design and build of new services and operational practices; contributing to Service Design, Service Transition or Continual Service Improvement projects, such as upgrades or server consolidation
- Assisting with most service management processes, helping to define standards and tools, and undertaking activities such as the evaluation of change requests, provision of second- and higher-level support, and the definition of coding systems for use in Incident and Problem Management
- Assisting with the management of contracts and vendors in support of Service Level Management and Supplier Management.

Technical Management organization

Technical Management is not normally provided by a single department or group. In all but the smallest organizations, where a single combined team or department may suffice, separate teams or departments will be needed for each type of infrastructure being used.

The primary criterion of Technical Management organizational structure is that of specialization or division of labour, where people are grouped according to their technical skill sets, determined by the technology that needs to be managed.

Examples of typical Technical Management teams or departments include Mainframe, Server (split by technology type, e.g. Unix server, Wintel server), Storage, Network, Desktop, Database, Directory Services, Internet or Web, Messaging and IP telephony.

3.7.3 Application Management

Application Management is responsible for managing applications throughout their lifecycle. Application Management supports the organization's business processes by helping to identify functional and manageability requirements for application software, and plays an important role in the design, testing and improvement of applications that form part of IT services. As such, it may be involved in development projects, but is not usually the same as the Applications Development team.

Application Management plays a role in all applications, whether purchased or developed in-house. Application Management plays the same dual role as Technical Management, i.e.:

- It is the custodian of technical knowledge and expertise related to managing applications
- It provides the actual resources to support the ITSM Lifecycle.

In addition to these high-level roles, Application Management also performs the following two specific roles:

- Providing guidance about how best to carry out the ongoing operational management of applications
- Integrating the Application Management Lifecycle into the ITSM Lifecycle.

It is common in many organizations to refer to applications as 'services'; however, applications are but one component of many needed to provide a service.

Application Management principles

- **Build or buy?** – One of the key decisions in Application Management is whether to buy an application that supports the required functionality, or to build the application specifically for the organization's requirements. These decisions are often made by a senior person, such as the Chief Technical Officer (CTO) or Steering Committee, but they are dependent on information from a number of sources.

  Application Management contributes to these decisions by helping with application sizing and workload forecasts, the specification of manageability requirements, and the identification of ongoing operational costs, etc.

- **Operational Models** – An Operational Model is the specification of the operational environment in which the application will run when it goes live. This is used during testing and transition phases to simulate and evaluate the live environment. The Operational Model should be defined and used in testing during the Service Design and Service Transition phases, respectively.

Application Management lifecycle

The lifecycle followed to develop and manage applications is referred to by many names, e.g. the Software Lifecycle (SLC) and the Software Development Lifecycle (SDLC). These are generally used by Applications Development teams, and examples of these approaches include Structured Systems Analysis and Design Methodology (SSADM) and Dynamic Systems Development Method (DSDM).

ITIL is primarily interested in the overall management of applications as part of IT services, whether they are developed in-house or purchased from a third party. For this reason, the term Application Management Lifecycle has been used, as it implies a more holistic view. This does not replace the SDLC, but it does mean that there should be greater alignment between the development view of applications and the 'live' management of those applications.

Figure 3.7 illustrates the Application Management Lifecycle, the key stages of which are summarized below.

- **Requirements** – Requirements for a new application are gathered, based on the business needs of the organization. This phase is active primarily during the Service Design phase of the ITSM Lifecycle.
- **Design, build, deploy** – Design includes the design of the application itself, and the design of the environment or operational model that the application has to run on.

  In the build phase, the application and operational model are made ready for deployment. Application components are coded or acquired, integrated and tested. For purchased software, this phase will include the actual purchase of the software and any customization required.

  Both the operational model and the application are then moved into production during the deploy phase, which is carried out by the Release and Deployment Management process, defined in the Service Transition stage of the lifecycle.

- **Operate, optimize** – In the operate phase, the IT services organization operates the application as part of delivering a service to the business. The performance of the application in relation to the overall service is measured continually against the Service Levels and key business drivers.

  In the optimize phase, the results of Service Level performance measurement are analysed and acted upon. Possible improvements to improve service levels or lower costs are initiated if necessary.

Figure 3.7 Application Management Lifecycle

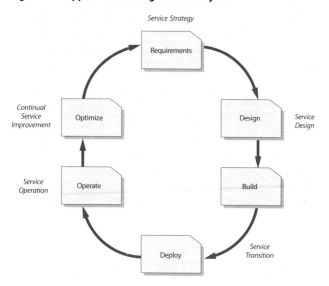

Application Management organization

Although all Application Management departments, groups or teams
perform similar activities, each application or set of applications has a
different set of management and operational requirements. The activities
to manage these applications are generic, but the specific schedule of
activities and the way they are performed will be different. For this reason,
Application Management teams and departments tend to be organized
according to the categories of applications that they support, e.g. financial
applications, business-specific applications (e.g. health care, insurance,
banking), online shopping, etc.

Traditionally, Application Development and Management teams and departments have been autonomous units. Each manages their own environment in their own way and has a separate interface to the business. These two worlds are being brought together by recent moves to Object Oriented and Service Oriented Architecture (SOA) approaches, together with growing pressure from the business to be more responsive and easy to work with.

This means that Application Development have greater accountability for the successful operation of applications they design, while Application Management have greater involvement in the development of applications. This does not change the fundamental role of each group, but it does require a more integrated approach to the SDLC.

Application Management and Application Development are involved in each stage of the Application Management Lifecycle and both groups are subordinate to the Service Strategy of the organization, with their efforts coordinated through Service Transition.

3.7.4   IT Operations Management

IT Operations Management is the function responsible for the ongoing management and maintenance of an organization's IT infrastructure in order to deliver the agreed level of IT services to the business. This is done according to performance standards defined during Service Design.

IT Operations Management includes two functions:

- ■ **IT Operations Control** – Generally staffed by shifts of operators and carries out routine operational tasks; IT Operations Control also provides centralized monitoring and control activities, usually using an operations bridge or Network Operations Centre.

  In addition to executing routine tasks and maintenance activities on behalf of Technical or Application Management teams, IT Operations

Control also performs a number of specific tasks, such as console management and job scheduling, summarized in section 3.6.

■ **Facilities management** – Responsible for the management of the physical IT environment, typically a data centre or computer rooms and recovery sites. Facilities management also includes the coordination of large-scale projects, e.g. data centre consolidation or server consolidation projects.

In some cases, the management of a data centre is outsourced, in which case facilities management has a role in the management of the outsourcing contract.

The activities performed by facilities management are summarized in section 3.6.

As with many ITSM processes and functions, IT Operations Management plays a dual role:

■ Execution of the activities and performance standards defined during Service Design and tested during Service Transition.

In this sense, IT Operations' role is primarily to maintain the status quo. The stability of the IT infrastructure and consistency of IT services is a primary concern of IT Operations. Even operational improvements are often aimed at finding simpler and better ways of doing the same thing.

■ Adding value to the different lines of business and supporting the value network (see the ITIL *Service Strategy* publication).

The ability of the business to meet its objectives and to remain competitive depends on the output and reliability of the day-to-day operation of IT. As such, IT Operations Management must be able to adapt continually and reliably to changing business requirements and demand.

In addition to IT Operations Management's objective of providing stability, focus is also given to:

- Regular scrutiny and improvements to achieve improved service at reduced costs
- Swift application of operational skills to diagnose and resolve any IT operations failures.

IT Operations Management organization

IT Operations Management is seen as a function in its own right but, in many cases, staff from Technical and Application Management groups form part of this function.

This means that some Technical and Application Management departments or groups will manage and execute their own operational activities. Others will delegate these activities to a dedicated IT Operations department.

3.8 PLANNING AND IMPLEMENTING SERVICE OPERATION

Service Operation is a phase in a lifecycle and not an entity in its own right. By the time a service, process, organization structure or technology is operating, it has already been implemented. In order to deliver stable IT services and deliver expected business outcomes, there are a number of processes and functions described in this publication that need to be formally implemented or otherwise addressed.

In addition, there are a number of generic implementation considerations to be addressed. These are summarized below.

Managing change in Service Operation

Service Operation should strive to achieve stability – but not stagnation. There are many valid and advantageous reasons why 'change is a good thing', but Service Operation staff must ensure that changes are absorbed without adverse impact on the stability of the services.

There are many things that may trigger a change in the Service Operation environment. These include new or upgraded components, legislative or regulatory changes, business changes, process enhancements, etc. Service Operation staff must be involved in all stages of such changes, from early planning through authorization, deployment and the measurement of success.

Planning and implementing service management technologies

There are a number of factors that organizations need to plan for during deployment and implementation of ITSM support tools. These include:

- Licensing
- Capacity requirements
- Timing and staff readiness
- Method of introduction – 'big bang' or phased.

3.9   CHALLENGES, OPPORTUNITIES AND OPTIMIZATION

Service Operation has a number of challenges that it must overcome in order to deliver reliably services that meet the needs of the business.

It can be difficult to get funding for Service Operation as the business can see the value of new services, but may consider Service Operation spending to be 'infrastructure costs' with no new functionality to show for the investment. This can be overcome by proper financial analysis that shows a positive return on investment (ROI).

Traditionally, there has been a separation between Service Operation staff and staff developing new services. This lack of engagement with development and project staff may lead to poor consideration of operational needs during design, and service management requirements not being addressed until too late.

Differences between Service Operation and Service Design can lead to further challenges, such as:

- Service Design typically focuses on individual projects; Service Operation considers all services together. This difference in perspective must be understood and managed to ensure that all services can be managed effectively and efficiently.
- Service Design projects have a start and end date; Service Operation focuses on ongoing processes and activities. This can make it difficult for Operation staff to take part in projects, and Design staff may move on before Operation staff are ready to take responsibility. This requires careful planning on both sides and Early Life Support (ELS) for new and change services.
- Service Design metrics tend to include project completion to time, budget and specification; Service Operation metrics focus on delivery of reliable cost-effective services. It may be difficult to predict the cost of running a service during design and to budget correctly for ongoing support. This should be addressed by involving Service Operation staff in Service Design and Transition activities.
- Many organizations have very limited Service Transition, with a change control process that simply schedules the deployment of changes after they have been designed. It is essential that Service Transition practices are followed and that Service Operation staff have the authority to reject changes that pose a significant risk.

Meeting these challenges requires integration of processes across the service lifecycle, with Service Operation staff being fully engaged during Service Design and Service Transition.

Service Operation needs to have good metrics to ensure that they know what is required and can demonstrate what they are achieving. Metrics depend on having good Service Level Management in place, and on effective Continual Service Improvement. Service Operation staff need to engage with staff in these areas to help ensure that suitable metrics are in place.

There are many organizational issues that can lead to challenges for Service Operation. Although some teams need to have a technology focus, others need to focus on particular processes, or particular services. This can result in a complex matrix of responsibilities. Knowledge Management and mapping of authority structures can help control complex organizations.

3.10   KEY MESSAGES AND LESSONS

- Success in Service Operation depends on achieving the correct balance between the conflicting priorities of internal and external views; stability and responsiveness; quality and cost; and reactive and proactive behaviour.
- Service Operation staff need to be involved and engaged in all phases of the lifecycle; this can help to ensure successful design, transition and improvement of services, with suitable metrics and operational features so that Service Operation staff are able to meet the business needs.
- Understanding the difference between events, Incidents, Service Requests, Access Requests and Problems is essential so that each of these can be handled correctly. It is also important that these processes work together, ideally using a single, integrated toolset, to enable best use of time and resources.
- The various functions involved in Service Operation may have overlapping or conflicting goals and activities. Roles and responsibilities must be defined in a way that ensures these are all clearly understood.
- There must be a balance of the needs of the development and operational activities: you cannot just focus on existing services, you have to also look at future services and support their implementation and plan for them (Service Transition).
- It must be clear what the operational requirements are so that new services can be designed and implemented effectively and efficiently.